I0116006

What are Species

What are Species

Nature and Human Studies Collection

LM Publishers

Introduction[1]

The term "species" was thus defined by the celebrated botanist De Candolle: "A species is a collection of all the individuals which resemble each other more than they resemble anything else, which can by mutual fecundation produce fertile individuals, and which reproduce themselves by generation, in such a manner that we may from analogy suppose them all to have sprung from one single individual." And the zoologist Swainson gives a somewhat similar definition: "A species, in the usual

---

[1] Based on the work of Alfred Russel Wallace, in *Darwinism,* 1889.

acceptation of the term, is an animal which, in a state of nature, is distinguished by certain peculiarities of form, size, colour, or other circumstances, from another animal. It propagates, 'after its kind,' individuals perfectly resembling the parent; its peculiarities, therefore, are permanent."

To illustrate these definitions we will take two common English birds, the rook (Corvus frugilegus) and the crow (Corvus corone). These are distinct *species*, because, in the first place, they always differ from each other in certain slight peculiarities of structure, form, and habits, and, in the second place, because rooks always produce rooks, and crows produce crows, and they do not interbreed. It was therefore concluded that all the rooks in the world had descended from a single pair of rooks, and the crows in like manner from a single pair of crows, while it was considered impossible that crows could have descended from rooks or *vice versâ*. The "origin" of the first pair of each kind was a mystery. Similar remarks may be applied to our two common plants, the sweet violet (Viola odorata) and the dog violet (Viola canina). These also produce their like and never produce each other or intermingle, and they were therefore each supposed to have sprung from a single individual whose "origin" was unknown. But besides the crow and the rook there are about thirty other kinds of birds in various parts of the world, all so much like our species that they receive the common name of crows; and some of them differ less from each other than does our crow from our rook. These are all *species* of the genus Corvus, and were therefore believed to have been always as distinct as they are now, neither more nor less, and to have each descended from one pair of ancestral crows of the same identical species, which themselves had an unknown "origin." Of violets there are more than a hundred different kinds in various parts of the world, all differing very slightly from each other and forming distinct *species* of the genus Viola. But, as these also each produce their like and do not intermingle, it was believed that every one of them had always been as distinct from all the others as it is now, that all the individuals of each kind had descended from one ancestor, but that the "origin" of these hundred slightly differing ancestors was unknown. In the words of Sir John Herschel, quoted by Mr. Darwin, the origin of such species was "the mystery of mysteries."

What are Species?[2]

In its most general acceptation the word "species" signifies a kind or sort of something, which something is the *genus* to which the species belongs. Thus, a black stone is a species of the genus stone; a gray horse is a species of the genus horse; a scalene triangle is a species of the genus triangle; and, generally, it may be said that every adjective denotes a species of the genus indicated by the substantive to which it is applied.

In the technology of the physical sciences the term "species" has a more

---

[2] by Thomas H. Huxley.

restricted signification. It is used to denote a group of individuals which corresponds with an early stage of that process of abstraction by which the qualities of individual objects are arranged in the subordinated categories of classification.

The individual object alone exists in Nature; but, when individual objects are compared, it is found that many agree in all those characters which, for the particular purpose of the classifier, are regarded as important, while they differ only in those which are unimportant; and those which thus agree constitute a species, the definition of which is a statement of the common characters of the individuals which compose the species.

Again, when the species thus established are compared, certain of them are found to agree with one another, and to differ from all the rest in some one or more peculiarities. They thus form a group, which, logically, is merely a species of higher order, while technically it is termed a "genus." And, by a continuation of the same process, genera are grouped into families, families into orders, and so on. Each of the groups thus named is in the logical sense a genus, of which the next lower groups constitute the species.

The characters on which species are based necessarily depend upon the nature of the bodies classified. Thus, mineral species are founded upon purely morphological characters; that is to say, they are defined by peculiarities either of form, color, and the like, or of structure, which last term may be used to include both the physical and the chemical characteristics of a mineral. The distinction between a species and a variety is wholly arbitrary, except so far as it is commonly agreed that individuals which differ from others only as terms of a gradual series of modifications belong to the same species, and are to be considered merely as varieties of that species.

It is conceivable that animals and plants should have been known to us only by their remains preserved in museums or in the fossil state. If this had been the case, biological, like mineralogical species, could have been defined only by morphological characters; that is to say, by the peculiarities of their outward form and inward structure; and, as a matter of fact, this is the state of our knowledge in respect of a large proportion of the existing fauna and flora of the world, and of all extinct animals and plants.

A botanist or a conchologist who sets to work to arrange a newly-received collection sorts his plants or his shells out according to their likenesses and unlikenesses of form and structure, until he has arranged them into groups of individuals which agree in certain constant characters and differ only by insignificant features, or by such peculiarities as vary in different individuals in such a manner that an insensible gradation can be traced between those forms which have the peculiarity strongly marked and those in which it is absent.

Thus far the considerations which guide the biologist in the establishment of species differ in no respect from those which influence the mineralogist.

But although naturalists have no more direct knowledge of any but the morphological character of the great majority of the species of animals and plants than they would have of so many mineral specimens, they are familiar with many animals and plants in the living state when they exhibit phenomena to which the mineral world presents no parallel, and the study of these phenomena of active life has complicated the conception of species in biology, by adding physiological to morphological considerations.

The fact that living beings originate by generation from other living beings is one of the circumstances in their history which most completely differentiates them from minerals. This process of generation enters in various ways into the conception of biological species.

For example, it is a generally assumed axiom in biology that whatever proceeds from a living being by way of generation is of the same species as that from which it proceeds, whether the morphological differences between parent and offspring be great or small. The two sexes are often extraordinarily different, and in cases of the so-called alternation of generation the successive zoöids may differ very widely; but, inasmuch as the differing forms in these cases proceed from the same parents, no one doubts that they belong to the same species. The breeds of domesticated animals and plants often differ morphologically as widely as admitted species, but, apart from other considerations, historical evidence that they have the same parentage suffices to cause them to be regarded as of one species. It is not quite clear that the converse of the axiom which has just been referred to would be admitted, and that living beings which arise from totally distinct parents are of different species, even though morphologically identical. The wellnigh exploded hypothesis of the multiplicity of centres of origin for species of wide distribution implies the belief that groups of individuals which have proceeded from distinctly-created parents may, nevertheless, be of the same species, while the supporters of the no less nearly extinct hypothesis of the independent creation of the fauna and flora of successive formations used to affirm that, although indistinguishable, two forms from separate formations must be of distinct species, because they had been created separately. However, these subtleties have ceased to have any practical importance.

In the next place it is observed that, while individuals of the same morphological species breed freely with one another and give rise to perfectly fertile offspring, the unions of individuals of different morphological species are, as a rule, either unfertile or imperfectly fertile. Thus fertility, like parentage, has become a physiological character of species; and, though in the case of some domesticated animals, as pigeons, the extreme forms are more different from one another than many morphological species, yet they, apart from the historical evidence of their parentage, are held to be members of the same species, because they are all perfectly fertile one with another, and their offspring are also perfectly fertile.

Thirdly, it is a matter of experience that, as a general rule, and taking the whole cycle of forms through which a living being runs into account, offspring and parent are so similar that they belong to one and the same morphological species; and it is further in evidence that many species have endured for extremely long periods without any notable difference being discernible between ancestor and descendant. Moreover, in some cases, varieties are found to revert to the character of the species from which they have proceeded. The conclusion has been drawn that the character of species is physiologically fixed; that is to say, that, however long the process of generation may be continued, the individuals either retain the identical morphological character of the oldest ancestor, or, if they vary, the varieties remain fertile with one another.

Assuming that species have the physiological character thus enumerated, certain conclusions respecting the "origin of species" are inevitable. It is clear that no existing species can have arisen by the intercrossing of preexisting species, or by the variation of preexisting species, but that every species must have existed from all eternity, or have come into existence suddenly in its present form, which is the objective fact denoted by what is termed creation.

At the dawn of modern biology, a century ago, no scientific evidence respecting the real history of life on the globe was extant, and, for any proof that existed to the contrary, species might have been of eternal duration. But philosophical speculation combined with theological dogma not only to favor the contrary opinion, but to lead the most philosophic naturalist of his day to embody the hypothesis of creation in a definition of species. "Totidem numeramus species quot in principio formæ sunt creatæ" (we reckon as many species as there were forms created in the beginning) is the well-known formula of Linnæus.

In practice Linnæus regarded species from a purely mythological point of view; in theory, he assumed the common ancestry and the limited variability of species, though he was disposed to allow more freedom in this direction than most of his successors. On the other hand, he seems to have attached comparatively little weight to the assumed sterility of hybrids, and to have held a sort of modified doctrine of evolution, supposing that existing species may have been produced by the interbreeding of comparatively few primordial forms.

It is mainly to the influence of Cuvier's authority that we owe the general acceptance of the views respecting the physiological character of species, which up till within the last few years have been almost universally prevalent.

In the introduction to the "*Règne Animal*" (1816), Cuvier writes:

"There is no proof that all the differences which now distinguish organized beings are such as may have been produced by circumstances. All that has been advanced upon this subject is hypothetical; experience seems to show, on the contrary, that, in the actual state of things, varieties are confined within rather narrow limits, and, so far as we can retrace antiquity, we perceive that these limits were the same as at present.

"We are thus obliged to admit of certain forms, which since the origin of things have been perpetuated, without exceeding these limits; and all the beings appertaining to one of these forms constitutes what is termed a species. Varieties are accidental subdivisions of species.

"Generation being the only means of ascertaining the limits to which varieties may extend, species should be defined, the reunion of individuals descended from one another, or from common parents, or from such as resemble them as closely as they resemble each other; but, although this definition is vigorous, it will be seen that its application to particular individuals may be very different when the necessary experiments have been made."

It need hardly be said, however, that in practice Cuvier founded his species upon purely and exclusively morphological characters, just as his predecessors and successors have done. The combination of Cuvier's views on the fixity of species with the discovery of the succession of life on the globe, which was so largely the result of his labors, led his successors into curious difficulties. Developing the fundamental idea of the "Discours sur les Révolutions de la Surface du Globe," naturalists were forced to conclude not only that existing species are the result of creation, but that the creative act by which they were brought into being was only the last repetition of a series of such acts by which the often depopulated world has been as frequently repeopled, and thus orthodox belief respecting the existing flora and fauna led to a terribly heterodox cosmogony.

The contemporary and countryman of Cuvier, Lamarck, must be regarded as the chief founder of the reaction against the doctrines which Cuvier advocated—a reaction which, overpowered and disregarded for many years, has acquired such force since and through the publication of the "Origin of Species," that it has almost swept opposition away. Lamarck's vast acquaintance with the details of invertebrate zoology rendered him familiar with the great variability of many species, and led him to see that variation is in some way related to change of conditions; the frequent occurrence of transitional forms between apparently distinct species, when large suites of specimens (especially when they are obtained from different parts of a wide geographical area) are examined, tended to bring into strong light the tenuity of the distinction between species and varieties. The fact of embryology, the occurrence of rudimentary organs, and the fundamental unity of structure which obtains in vast groups, such as the vertebrata and arthropoda, all tended to suggest the existence of a genetic connection between species, so that Lamarck was finally led to renounce the doctrine of the fixity of species, and to define a species as "a collection of individuals which resemble each other and produce their like by generation, so long as the surrounding conditions do not alter to such an extent as to cause their habits, characters, and forms, to vary."

According to this definition the distinction between species and variety once more becomes conventional. A variety is, in fact, a nascent species; and the notion of the creation of species vanishes, inasmuch as every species is the result of the modification of a predecessor. Lamarck's views of the nature of geological changes were in harmony with his biological speculations, and wholesale catastrophic revolutions were as completely excluded from the one as from the other.

It is impossible to read the "*Discours sur les Révolutions*" of Cuvier, and the "*Principes*" of Lamarck, without being struck with the superiority of the former in sobriety of thought, precision of statement, and coolness of judgment. And it is no less impossible to consider the present state of biological science without being impressed by the circumstance that it is the conception of Lamarck which has triumphed, and that of Cuvier which has been utterly vanquished.

Catastrophic geology has vanished out of sight, and is everywhere replaced by the conception of slow and gradual change. With it has disappeared the once prevalent notion that the whole living population of the earth has been swept away and replaced in successive epochs. On the contrary, it is now well established that the changes which have taken place in that population have been effected by the slow and gradual substitution of species for species.

Moreover, it is well established that in some cases the succession of forms in time is the same as that which should have occurred if the hypothesis of evolution is correct.

The rapid advance of comparative anatomy has diminished or removed the wide intervals which formerly appeared to separate the different divisions of the animal and vegetable kingdoms from one another. Even the hiatus between the vertebrata and the invertebrata is bridged over by recent discovery. The establishment of the cell-theory, however much the views originally propounded by Schwann have been modified, leaves no doubt that there is a fundamental similarity in minute structure, not only between all animals, but between them and plants, while the discoveries of embryologists have proved that even the most complex forms of living beings do, in the course of their development, run through a series of changes of the same order as those which are postulated by the evolution-theory for life in time.

Again, the facts of geographical distribution, as now known, are absolutely incompatible with the hypothesis that existing animals and plants have migrated from a common centre, whether Mount Ararat or any other; and, by demonstrating the similarity of the existing fauna and flora of any locality to that which inhabited the same area in the immediately precedent epoch, have furnished a strong argument in favor of the modifiability of species. Thus, it is not too much to say that the facts of biology known at the present day are all consistent with and in favor of the view of species entertained by Lamarck, while they are unfavorable to, if not incompatible with, those advocated by Cuvier; and that, even if no suggestion has been offered, or could be offered, as to the causes which have led to the gradual evolution of species, the hypothesis that they have arisen by such a process of evolution would be the only one which would have any scientific foundation.

The great service which has been rendered to science by Mr. Darwin, in the "Origin of Species" is that, in the first place, he has marshaled the ascertained facts of biology in such a manner as to render this conclusion irresistible; and, secondly, that he has proved the following proposition: Given, the existence of living matter endowed with variability, the interaction of variation with the conditions of existence must tend to give rise to a differentialism of the living matter into forms having the same morphological relations as are exhibited by the varieties and species which actually exist in Nature.

What is needed for the completion of the theory of the origin of species is, first, definite proof that selective breeding is competent to convert permanent races into physiologically distinct species; and, secondly, the elucidation of the nature of variability. It is conceivable that both the tendency to vary and the directions in which that tendency takes effect are determined by the molecular constitution of a living body, in which case the operation of the changes of external conditions will be indirect, and, so to speak, permissive. It is conceivable, on the other hand, that the tendency to vary is both originated and directed by the influence of external conditions, while it is also conceivable that both variation and the direction which variation takes are partly determined by intrinsic and partly by extrinsic conditions.

On the Origin of Species[3]

To answer this question (what are species?) is as difficult now as it was in the days of Linnaeus. Formerly it was supposed that a certain number of forms had been created, and that these, obeying natural laws as yet undiscovered, had split up and so given rise to groups, which afterwards were called genera. Such genera were clover, rose and buttercup, plums, apples and pears. Among them, by the addition of a name, certain species were distinguished, such as red clover, white clover, etc.

---

[3] by Hugo de Vries.

Linnaeus, in his first publications, adopted the above view. 'Each genus is created as such,' is one of his best known theses. Later he changed this in so far as to declare species created, i.e., those species which he recognized as such, and which he had endowed with binomials. In this manner, the power to split up, to produce new forms, and thus to form groups, was transferred to the species, which offered the great advantage, that, since species greatly surpassed the genera in number, the necessary number of splittings was correspondingly reduced.

Next to the disciples of Linnaeus and a few others who still adhered to the old doctrine, there soon arose a group of botanists and zoologists who went much farther in applying the principle of Linnaeus than was intended by him. The former continued to consider genera as created, and species to have originated from them. When the number of known species increased and soon assumed undreamed of proportions, it seemed but natural not to accept for each species a separate creation. But the others denied the possibility of a transition from an old form to a new one by natural means. Each actually existing form, constant from seed, must, according to their idea, have been created as such. They denied the right to collect groups of forms under one specific name, as did Linnaeus and, after him, his disciples, especially when, owing to constant research, an exceedingly large number of forms became known. Instead, they recognized each form as a unity — unities which could be collected under a generic name only.

But Linnaeus, guided more by the talents of a lawyer than by those of an investigator, had once for all connected his conception of a species with the use of the binomials introduced by him. Whatever bears two names is a species. This is the law which all must obey. Genera bear simple names, subdivisions of species tri -or quadrinomials. Whoever wishes to have a form recognized as a species, must give it two names. Unless this be done he will not attain his object. But the number of simple forms, constant from seed, increased year by year and, even for Europe alone, threatened to become ten times greater than it had been.

Since the validity of the theory of descent has been generally recognized, these questions have lost much of their importance.

The work of Darwin embraces two main theses which as a rule are not sufficiently distinguished and which even by him were frequently collated. The one was to ascertain the common descent of plants and animals, the other, to find how one species could have originated from another. These two points are mutually independent, and were especially so at the time of publication of Darwin's 'Origin of Species.'

The doctrine of the common descent of all organisms holds that genera, families and even the larger divisions of the plant-and animal-kingdoms originated in a manner identical with the one which, before the days of Linnæus, was largely accepted for the splitting of genera into species and afterwards for the formation of subspecies from species. The common origin of groups of smaller types was recognized; but how large these groups were no one knew exactly. Darwin extended their limits so as to enclose all living organisms, practically collecting them into a single genus.

For this purpose it was not even necessary to know how the simple forms themselves originated. What was conceded for these by everyone, had only to be applied to the larger groups. Yet Darwin attached considerable weight to this question and threw much light upon it.

That the smaller species are created as such is the view now held by a comparatively small group of scientists. It is a contention, the truth of which has never been generally recognized, and at the present time has of course lost all right of existence. Before and after Linnaeus, before and after Darwin, the formation of the smaller species, the one from the other, has, except by the few above mentioned, been generally recognized, a recognition based upon experience as well as on tradition.

The smaller species are called subspecies or, as in horticulture, varieties, and are therefore considered as subdivisions of the species of Linnaeus.

Their descent from other species was conceded even before the days of Darwin, but nothing was known regarding the manner of their origin. It was generally deemed sufficient to attribute it to environmental influence. In agriculture and in horticulture it occurred from time to time that new forms originated from older ones; it always happened unexpectedly and without gradual transitions, always by skips and jumps. The new forms were called sports; whether in nature the same thing occurred was unknown.

Both in agriculture and horticulture these sudden changes were very rare and always shrouded in mystery. They occurred without any apparent preparation, the new form appeared unexpectedly, and once its presence had become apparent it was impossible to trace its origin. One could but state the fact, which, for cultivation-and trade-purposes, was deemed quite sufficient; but its nature remained wrapped in darkness. Truly no tempting basis on which to found a grand theory.

It was for this reason that Darwin preferred to turn to more generally known, or, at least, more tangible, facts. He laid much stress on over-production, on the struggle for life which must be the consequence, and on the greater chances of success possessed by the strongest individuals or by those best adapted to their surroundings.

He pointed to the dissimilarity, the so-called variability of individuals, and showed it might be met with everywhere and at all times, in all organs and in all characters. This dissimilarity is decisive in the struggle for life; not in every individual case of course, for here chance plays too prominent a part, but in the majority of cases and in the long run.

That which is not fitted for the surroundings must succumb; each species adapts itself more or less to its environment; each species is different in nature from what it would be in the absence of all disturbing influences and were its reproduction unhampered.

How far can variability extend its influence? Has variability its limits? May variability proceed for centuries in the same direction or must it necessarily return to the starting point? Can variability bring about the formation of new characters or new organs or is it limited to differences in the degree of development of those already extant? Most of these questions were left unanswered at the time and, for the greater part, have remained so. And, as long as no answer was forthcoming, imagination had free play as regards the manner in which one species originated from another.

A stop was put to this when Quetelet discovered his famous law. Variability obeys certain rules; nothing outside the compass of these rules can be attributed to it. Variability is not unlimited and always returns to its starting point. There may be various causes for a prolonged deviation of variability from the mean, of which continued selection of individuals, strongly developed in any particular direction, is the most important; but as soon as these causes cease to exist or this selection ceases to be practiced, it must return to the mean. Variability is nothing but a more or less, a plus-variation or a minus-variation; it does not go in any direction other than the greater or lesser development of a character already present. Variability merely causes a decrease or an increase; it does not create.

It remained for the disciples of Quetelet to draw attention to the consequences of his discovery, which are among the most recent results of scientific research. Darwin and Wallace were not acquainted with these objections to their theory, it was only long after the publication of their works, that science became aware of the existence of these objections and of their importance.

The theory of variability, such as we know it at the present day, does not lead to conclusions favorable to the theory of the gradual origin of species, the theory which assumes that species originated by a gradual increase in the degree of variability. Hence many writers have at various times declared more or less openly against this theory. Others again have tried to reconcile it with the newly discovered facts. But Darwin's explanation is a most plausible one, which, apparently at least, solves all difficulties. And the voice of his antagonists is as yet not so powerful but that the great majority should remain faithful to the old banner.

Besides, Darwin never expressed himself so definitely upon this point as some would have us believe. Openly in one passage, less so in a second one, he acknowledges the possibility of another explanation. It might very well be possible that the changes of the species in nature might occur suddenly, as had been observed to be the case in agriculture and horticulture. This would, as satisfactorily as the theory of gradual change, explain the relationship existing between smaller species in nature and more especially between those agricultural plants which systematic botany unites into a single species. Without a doubt, the formation of the various kinds of beets, of oats or of barley, would have required many centuries, but the results are accounted for as easily by accepting exceedingly slow changes as the causes of the formation of species, as they would be were we to consider them due to shocks occurring but once in a protracted period. Darwin fully realized this and considered the doubt upon this subject as one of the weakest points of his theory.

Darwin, as did many since, compared the origin of species in nature to the methods, ordinarily used in agriculture, to obtain improved races of plants and animals. On this subject much confusion exists. Horses, for instance, are improved principally by crossing with specimens of a superior race, which specimens more or less fully transfer the good qualities of the race to the descendants. But it is certain that in nature the species did not originate in this manner, at least not as a general rule. Improved races are obtained only by careful and constant selection in one direction. This bears a great resemblance to the origin of species, but there is this objection, that such a race would never be independent of selection; as soon as selection ceases, the good qualities disappear.

Species and subspecies, even true varieties, on the other hand, are totally independent of the mother species; neither in nature nor in cultivation do they return to the old type, either by a change in environmental conditions or by the cessation of a selection; always provided of course, that accidental crossing is impossible.

The experience yielded by agriculture would lead one to consider a gradual transition from one species into another improbable. They point to a distinct difference between gradually improved races and those suddenly formed, so-called varieties. The former bear no resemblance, the others a resemblance in all respects to wild species.

During the last few decades several writers have expressed themselves more or less strongly against the conception of a gradual origin of species. In America

Cope was the one to set the example. Among paleontologists Dollo, among zoologists Bateson, and recently among botanists Korschinsky declared themselves in favor of the doctrine of the discontinuity of the natural ancestral trees. But their opinions have not been sharply defined and formulated and are based upon an acquaintance with facts not much larger than that commanded by Darwin himself. Hence their small influence and the small progress made by their convictions. Hence the American paleontologist Scott, a devoted adherent of Cope's doctrine, deemed it necessary to defend this doctrine against Bateson 's book. For his conception of discontinuity is entirely different from that of Bateson.

They are both dissatisfied with the reigning views on the origin of species by gradual variability, but in its place each wishes to put an entirely different conception.

It would lead too far were I to enter here upon the various points on which their theories differ; let it be sufficient to note some parts of Scott's treatise, since this gives the sharpest and clearest contrast to the reigning view. In the long ancestral trees which have been brought to light by the study of prehistoric animals, one form leads gradually to another. When the strata are sufficiently known there remain no breaks in the pedigree. Breaks are met with only where the strata are wanting or where it has as yet been impossible to study them thoroughly. Each ancestral tree consists of an uninterrupted series of forms. Between two adjacent ones there exists no greater difference than between the two most closely related species of the present day. And in the successive strata they follow each other up in such a manner as corresponds to the gradual development of the ancestral tree.

But how did each form originate from the one immediately preceding it? Gradually or suddenly?

Directly, paleontology can of course not teach us anything upon this subject. Did the species originate suddenly, then there can have been no intermediate forms, but even if they originated gradually the chances that such intermediate forms would have become fossilized, are exceedingly slight. For how small is the proportion of fossilized specimens to those which once must have existed! In any case, no such intermediate forms have been found, and it is for this reason that many paleontologists accept a sudden formation of new forms from the older ones.

The transition is slight, as slight for instance as the well-known differences between the local races of slugs; but as these races are constant, so in paleontology are the closest related forms sharply separated from one another.

The contrast between the views of Scott and those of the majority of botanists and zoologists has, I believe, been sufficiently shown here. According to Scott species did not originate gradually, but by small jumps. By each jump a limit was passed, but after that the species remained constant until, perhaps many centuries later, a new shock produced a new form.

Each species, each subspecies, or even each variety, is constant in all its characters; they remain the same from the beginning till the end, until, later on, either after having produced other species, or without having done so, they succumb in the struggle for life.

This theory restores the doctrine of the invariability of species to its old place. And this invariability is so general a matter of experience that it has always remained an exceedingly weak point of Darwin's theory of descent.

The continual, slow, even inappreciable changes of species, which Darwin, but more especially Wallace and his disciples, accepted, and which are so lineally opposed to every-day experience, do not exist for Scott. Each species remains unchanged as long as its period of existence lasts. All its characters vary more or less according to the law of Quetelet, but the type, to which all variations return, remains the same through centuries.

A species changes only when it produces others. Or rather, it does not change, but continues to exist next to the species newly formed. It may be compared to a tree, which, though it produces branches, does not cease growing in length. Only when among its descendants there are types better fitted for the battle of life, a species may locally succumb. But it would require a long time before the new species had entirely taken the place of the old.

It is clear that one must distinguish by some simple term variation by jumps from variation obeying the law of Quetelet. It is not practical to use the terms, sport, discontinuous variation or spontaneous variation, since they tend to produce the impression of something incomprehensible. Scott did not use these terms. He speaks of 'mutations.' A mutation occurs when one species is formed from another. As it is, 'mutation' is the expression in general use before the days of Darwin, and at first used by Darwin himself. Since it has apparently fallen into disuse, except in paleontology, where it is met with in various authors, always conveying the same meaning, it seems best to continue to use this term. Hence as long as species produce others they are called mutable, and this part of the doctrine of variability is known as mutability.

Once it has been conceded that species originate from others by mutation, one can go on to investigate what deductions must be made in regard to this process from the facts with which we are acquainted. And as long as an empirical investigation was impossible it was of the utmost importance to be able, even in this manner, to form an opinion about it.

First of all, we can come to the conclusion that mutations must be the smallest changes which can produce a difference between two species or rather between two constant types. Ordinarily the estimation of the differences existing between two related species is too great. Differences as between a horse and a donkey are of course not the result of a single mutation; there must have been a series of transition forms, at present extinct. Nobody will expect to see so great a change occur at once. Even much slighter differences, for instance those existing between our native violets, are still too large; here also there must have existed transition forms. And indeed a comparison with the floras of other countries actually does show a number of forms which bridge over these differences.

Yet differences between species are often so small that only a very careful study can make us acquainted with them. Among our native plants I have but to mention *Cochlearia Anglica* and *C. danica, Lepigonum [Spergularia] salinum* and *L. medium, Chrysanthemum maritimum* and *C. inodorum, Carex*

Oederi and *C. flava.* These are differences which one would rather neglect. Other examples can be met with in the genera *Rosa, Rubus, Salix, Hieracium* and many others; each botanist is acquainted with them, they are the common stumblingblocks on botanical excursions. Yet in systematic botany they are regularly recognized as *bona fide* species.

It sometimes occurs that two of these species which closely resemble each other grow side by side, as in the instances above-mentioned. In this case one can as a rule compare them when fresh, and in this manner fully realize the differences existing between them. But it happens far more frequently that the two plants, or three or four members of a small group, occur in different countries, often at great distances from one another. Then the differences are far less apparent. To this must be added that by the drying process necessary for herbarium purposes, many characters are lost. In that case the plants are no longer clearly distinguished, and are ordinarily considered as a single species, united under one name. This happens with *Draba verna, Viola tricolor, Helianthemum vulgare* and numerous other plants. It is only when we obtain them from different countries and grow them next to each other in the garden that the differences become apparent, and it is only then that these differences prove to be as great as those existing between the members of the above-mentioned couples of species.

One must therefore consider each mutation a step not greater than the differences between *Chrysanthemum inodorum* and *C. maritimum* for instance. I choose this example because the first species, the double form, with entirely filled, pure white, exceedingly graceful heads, is a well-known component of bridal bouquets. Besides, both are native species and of common occurrence, but generally not distinguished on botanical excursions. Where the differences between related species are greater, the lack of transition forms must be attributed to the fact that these live in other countries, or to their having become extinct.

In the second place, various investigators have come to the conclusion that mutations must occur periodically. For it is only in this manner that we can make the theory of descent agree with the undeniable fact that the species, such as we know them at present, have remained unchanged for centuries. In certain localities, on islands for instance, or places so situated that for centuries no transportation of plants or seeds can have taken place, the individuals of any one species do not show any or, at least, no constant differences, the above-mentioned couples of species, and compound species excepted. Spruces form a compound species, consisting of numerous types, but the common fir which without doubt is older than our era has remained the same everywhere. It is ever thus; the species do not undergo any gradual change, but each species is constant and remains so until others take its place. It never or but rarely occurs that new species make their appearance in fully investigated countries, unless indeed they happen to have been introduced from elsewhere. Yet it is probable that new species are formed quite frequently, but that, being too weak, they succumb before one becomes aware of their existence.

The numerous small species which are united under the name *Draba verna* are constant to seed, they do not change, besides they are distributed throughout Europe. It is therefore considered probable that there was a time during which they were formed, probably in a comparatively small region in the central part of Europe [at the present day they are most frequent along the Rhine and the Loire], and that in this locality flourished one or more species from which the present forms originated. At the end of this mutation-period the species would again have become constant. In this manner mutable and immutable periods in the development of species would have alternated more or less regularly.

There is a great tendency to consider a rapid increase in number as one of the reasons which cause a species to become temporarily mutable. Many species multiply exceedingly rapidly when they are transported to a new region where the conditions are favorable. Many European plants did this in America, likewise many American plants in Europe, as is only too well known through the waterpest, *Elodea canadensis.* As a matter of fact, we did not see them 'mutate,' but this may have been due to insufficient observation. It would be of great importance to pay close attention to this point when draining lakes, clearing waste lands, after forest fires and in similar cases.

Whether the mutations, during the mutable period, have been one-sided or many-sided, is a most important question and one frequently discussed by the adherents of the mutation theory.

The case of *Draba verna,* just mentioned, certainly speaks in favor of many-sided variability; the 200 'subspecies' known, vary in all organs and in all possible ways. Numerous other instances might be quoted. But opposed to them are the results obtained by paleontology. The progress in zoological times, more particularly in the animal kingdom, has always followed definite lines; by a straight line nature tried to reach her goal, not by zigzag lines, feeling her way. The main line has of course numerous small side branches, but branches which do not lead to still living types are rare. Scott and others deduce from this that mutability is one-sided, only progressing in the desired direction. Yet it might as well be possible that the mutations were many-sided, but that of them only those survived which excelled their ancestors in a particular direction, better fitting them for the existing conditions.

Finally one can come to a very important conclusion in regards the manner in which plants and animals mutate. It is this, that new species did not originate in a single individual, but in a number of individuals, either at the same time or during a number of years. Delboeuf was the first to formulate this idea, and Scott and others agree with him on this point.

This is a quite simple and natural view to take. A single individual would, among all the members of his former species, practically have no chance of life and reproduction, even if it were a hermaphrodite plant and much better adapted to local conditions than the others. For this chance plays too prominent a part in the struggle for life. There are a thousand chances that a seed does not germinate or is killed in its prime, independent of any qualities it may possess. Once the young plant has passed this period, the chances certainly are better, but even then many succumb because they occupy an unfavorable place. But when a plant produces a number of individuals of the new species at the same time, and repeats this for a number of years, then the chances of the new species are sufficient; and this even if it is weaker or in some regards inferior, and certainly if it is as good as the mother species. It is not at all necessary that the new species be stronger, or be at once offered the opportunity to make use of its superior qualities.

Delboeuf carefully calculated the chances, but even without these calculations one can see the truth of his remarks. For the larger the number of mutating individuals, and the more generations this mutating lasts, the greater will become the chance of the new species to maintain itself among the old one, always supposing the former is not so weak as to be crowded out each time. To be better equipped than others before entering upon the struggle for life is certainly a great advantage, but not a *sine quâ non* for ultimate success.

Reviewing the above, we find that the mutation theory comprises the following theses. Species originated from others by sudden but small changes, often so small as to be hardly visible to the neophyte. They are constant and true to seed from the first; neither are they connected with the mother species by a series of intermediate forms, nor do they have to pass in their prime, a stage of gradual development. This formation of new forms does not take place continually, but it is only from time to time that a species enters a period of mutability; in this case it produces, during a certain number of years, one or more, perhaps an exceedingly large number of new species. The mother species itself remains unchanged; it may persist after the mutable period is passed, and in that case retains its old characters.

The new species make their appearance in several, probably in numerous, individuals, and during each year of the mutation period. If they do not do this, their chances of life are exceedingly small, but in the other case their chances are sufficient, even if the new species are not in any regard superior to the mother species. The weaker ones among the new forms disappear of course very early.

The real struggle for life, in which natural selection must decide whether the young types shall continue to exist or not, only comes later on; it is not a war between species, but against other organisms, and against climate and soil.

In 1886, when I was preparing to write my *Intracellular Pangenesis,* the above mentioned considerations were only partly known to me. De Bary's studies on *Draba verna* only appeared in 1889, Bateson's book in 1894, Scott's article a little later, etc. But what was known at this time was sufficient to convince me that the formation of species should lend itself to experimental investigation. This was certainly directly opposed to the *reigning* opinion and especially the conception of a slow and gradual origin was not in favor of my view. It was thought that sudden transitions were limited to the so-called varieties, that they occurred in agriculture and horticulture only, and besides so rarely that an actual study of the problem was not to be thought of.

I then began a more systematic study of the variability of plants, a subject which always had possessed a great attraction for me. It very soon became apparent that observations in nature and in the garden could not lead to the desired goal. Even if one pays constant attention to the same individuals and the same localities, visiting them in various seasons and in different years, the observations remain too incomplete. This is but natural, since mutability commences with the seed and in nature but comparatively little seed, after germinating, attains its full development. I therefore decided to have recourse to sowing-experiments and for this purpose collected as much seed as possible from wild growing plants.

This seed was sown in my experimental garden, in some cases on quite a large scale. Besides I sowed seed gathered from some specimens of wild plants growing isolated in the garden. It was of course my aim to try to find among them one or more species which were passing through a mutation period. Among the seed sown was for instance that of *Verbascum thapsiforme, Thrincia hirta, Crepis biennis, Centaurea nigra, Capsella Bursa pastoris, Bidens cernua, Aster Tripolium, Cynoglossum officinale, Sisymbrium Alliaria, Daucus Carota,* and a number of other wild plants. As far as possible I allowed myself to be guided by symptoms of a particular tendency to variability, and hence chose by preference seed from plants with fasciated stems, split leaves or other variations. I also sowed, as far as room permitted, seed of annual garden plants, bought in shops.

It is clear that, notwithstanding the immense amount of work involved, the chances of success were exceedingly small. Yet I was lucky enough to find the very thing wanted. Among a hundred species there was a single one which proved to be mutable, at first but in a small degree, but sufficiently to decide me to abandon nearly all other experiments and to study this one plant as thoroughly as possible. Of the other species I had in the meantime obtained a number of monstrous races; these I continued to cultivate, but not the others.

The plant referred to was *Oenothera Lamarckiana,* a species of American origin, which has here escaped from cultivation, as did formerly both the evening primroses, *Oenothera biennis* and *Oenothera muricata,* which at the present time are quite common on our sand dunes. *Oenothera Lamarckiana,* the large evening primrose, surpasses both other "species in size of flowers, but for the rest is very much like them. This plant was first described by Lamarck as *Oenothera grandiflora,* but by this name a number of other species of *Oenothera* are known. Seringe changed the name to *Oenothera Lamarckiana,* which name has been retained.

In 1886 I collected a quantity of seed from wild plants of *Oenothera Lamarckiana* and also transported a number of rosettes of biennial specimens to the botanical garden at Amsterdam. The next year they flowered profusely and produced a large quantity of seed.

The seed obtained from wild plants was sown in 1887 and yielded at once what we desired. For among the plants obtained from it, there were three which, though agreeing among each other, possessed characters entirely deviating from those of the rest. This species was, therefore, able to produce at least one new form. The new form differed more from the mother species than the three species above mentioned did among each other. The leaves were broader, rounder and more obtuse, the buds swollen and the fruits small. The stems were small, weak and remained brittle even in autumn. At the tips of the branches the young leaves and buds were collected in crowded rosettes, so that at first the plants were denoted 'roundheads.' In a number of other particulars they differed more or less from the ordinary form, in fact they did not entirely agree with it in a single point. The most important difference, however, was the inability to produce good pollen. The anthers of the mother species are, when open, thickly covered with a sticky powder, which is entirely lacking in the case of the roundheads. The anthers of the new form are dry, what little pollen there is is shriveled, for the greater part unfertile and entirely unfit for fertilization. The plant is purely feminine. Male or hermaphrodite specimens I never saw, though I have often cultivated hundreds of roundheads. On account of the broad leaves, and thick buds,

Oenothera lata was chosen as the systematic name.

Encouraged by these results, I continued my investigation, partly, during the same year, by a closer study of the locality where the seed was collected, partly by sowing experiments on a large scale in the spring of the year following. The former made me acquainted with two new types, which had remained unobserved in 1886, but which, as rosettes of root-leaves, must have been present at the time, since *Oenothera Lamarckiana* is, in that locality, biennial, with hardly any exception. The one was glabrous, more delicate and more graceful, but as robust as the common form, the other had so short a style that the stigma, instead of protruding far above the stamens, was situated at the base of the flower. Both forms were formerly absolutely unknown, and, later on, in the sowing-experiments, proved to be as constant and true to seed as the mother species. That they originated in the locality where they were found may be considered as certain, but how this happened could not be investigated.

The seed, sown in the spring of the following year, again yielded two new forms. The one was a dwarf form, such a one as occurs from time to time among all kinds of culture plants—but a few decimeters high, whereas the mother species attains a height of $1\frac{1}{12}$ to 2 meters and more. The other was a form with shiny leaves, about half the size of *Oenothera Lamarckiana,* narrow, dark green, and very graceful. Both were quite fertile and produced a large quantity of seed.

Dwarf forms are ordinarily described along with the species to which they belong, as *varietas nana* or *nanella,* and my dwarf forms agree with them in every respect. They offer a good contrast with the other types, which cannot be termed varieties in the ordinary sense. For, in the first place, they deviate from the parent species not in a single character, but in all, and, in the second, they do not have their parallel in other genera. For repetition, such as appearance of white flowers, glabrous leaves, thornless stems and fruits, unbranched stems, variegated leaves, double flowers, etc., is one of the most common characteristics of true varieties.

Later the dwarfs proved to be constant to seed. Not so the shiny variety. Though I did not sow the latter each year, I did it frequently; its characters reappeared as a rule in but about one third of the individuals.

By sowing I obtained in 1888 nearly 15,000 plants, among which there were five dwarfs and five *latas,* that is to say, of each about 1 on every 3,000. In later years, when I became familiar with the most favorable methods of treatment, the percentage increased considerably, until at last there appeared approximately one new form on every 100 individuals.

The *latas* were, as we have seen, obtained partly from seed collected from wild plants and partly from seed yielded by wild plants transported to and cultivated in the botanic garden. Yet they agreed entirely in all respects, forming but a single well-defined type. Later in 1889 and in 1894, I also found them in the original locality. In my garden they made their appearance nearly every year. Each lata-plant which, without similar ancestors, originated from the *Oenothera Lamarkiana,* bears always exactly the same characters; one can always recognize it shortly after germination, and predict at the time all characters which it will exhibit later on. The same is true for the dwarfs, for the shiny forms, etc.

Once the certainty obtained of having found a mutating plant, I of course applied myself as closely as possible to a study of this phenomenon. Naturally this was at first connected with great difficulties, especially because I did not have an exact idea of what I was to look for. It was only in 1895 that I succeeded in surmounting these difficulties. I had by that time realized how small were the differences to which I had to pay attention, and that these differences, at least for the greater part, are apparent in the earliest stages of development. I therefore sowed on a large scale, reviewed my plants nearly daily, and changed each clearly deviating form to another bed, where it was given plenty of room and tended with great care.

That year I obtained about 14,000 plants from seed. Dwarfs and roundheads made their appearance in large numbers, 60 of the former and 73 of the latter. Their parents had been ordinary *Lamarckianas,* carefully pollinated with each other's pollen, as had been their ancestors of the last two generations and therefore of pure descent, as were probably all their ancestors of the original locality. The shiny form also made its appearance, again in but a single specimen. Besides there appeared five entirely new forms; three of these were separated as rosettes, one only showed itself to be a new form, when flowering, and the other only during the next year after hibernating.

The last two were rare, the one, *O. leptocarpa,* appeared in two specimens, the other, *O. gigas,* in a single individual. Both are at present constant to seed, absolutely unchangeable. The former is not beautiful, but ranker and taller than *O. Lamarkiana,* and flowers later in the season. *Oenothera gigas,* on the other hand, is a splendid, exceedingly robust plant, which, with a rich crown of very large flowers, easily excels the mother species.

The three others I denoted as 'red-nerved,' *O. rubrinervis,* 'white,' *O. albida,* and *O. oblonga.* They appeared respectively in 8, 15 and 176 specimens. The whites were very weak, and all of them died without flowering. But they reappeared each year, and in 1897 I succeeded in getting them to blossom. After that they proved to be constant and true to seed. The same is true for the red-nerved ones and for the *oblongas,* which are very typical and easily cultivated species.

Since 1895 I have each year sown *Oenothera Lamarckiana,* always taking care that the seed was pure. Fertilization was always artificial, with their own pollen, and with the exclusion of all insects. Yearly I had a thousand or more seedlings and regularly found among them a number of mutations. The new forms with which I already was acquainted reappeared each time; with a single exception no others have been added. The percentage of mutants remained the same each year, of course with slight variations.

Repeatedly I saw new species originate which either did not flower or were sterile or which on account of general weakness succumbed early in life. Some of these clearly originated several times, others so rarely that it was practically impossible to make a diagnosis. A few of these I also found in the original locality. Hence nature evidently makes besides species capable of existence also those which are not so.

The latter disappear very soon and hence are hardly ever seen; the former persist for a greater or smaller number of years.

The above may be considered sufficient to prove that the origin of species is a phenomenon falling entirely within the limits of ordinary observation. One has but to search his surroundings for a plant which happens to be passing through a mutation period to be able to study the entire process. Transportation to the garden only serves to make isolation of the plant possible; it but shows what happens in nature, but which there, on account of unfavorable conditions, is but seldom or imperfectly observed.

At the same time one sees that experiment, in this first example, confirms the deductions made a long time since from paleontological and biological data.

Delboeuf, as well as Scott, requires that each new species does not appear in a single specimen, but in a number of specimens, and not once but during a number of years. For only under these conditions are their chances sufficient. It is exactly this which happens with the *Oenotheras*. They are formed each year, 1 per 1,000 or 1 per 100, in any case in a sufficiently large number to fall within the requirements formulated by the savants just mentioned. They are with a single exception at once constant from seed, without ever returning to the type of the mother species; they would, by sufficient isolation, at once form groups of uniform individuals. Nothing indicates their appearance in advance, there is not even a hint of transition; once formed they are perfect, and retain, even after several generations, their original characters. They originate with a shock or jump and then are constant.

They are formed from the mother species as side issues, and not because the mother species undergoes a gradual change. On the contrary in nearly all mutations, the species continues unchanged, and to it belongs the great mass of individuals, until one day the struggle for life shall turn the scales.

Mutability is not one-sided, as many paleontological series would lead one to expect, but many-sided as must be deduced from the principles laid down by Darwin. And the new *Oenotheras* vary in different organs and in various directions; most frequently the new characters are injurious, sometimes indifferent, occasionally beneficial, probably at least. Next to strong new species there occur weak ones, next to these, those so weak as never to reach the flowering period; and finally sterile forms. From this array of forms nature, in the struggle for life, later on makes its choice; only those most fit continue to exist. Even here experiment confirms theory.

What is the duration of a mutation period? Geology answers: probably very long, for otherwise the chances of life of the new species would be too small. And it seems to me that in the case of *Oenothera Lamarckiana* I have seen neither the beginning nor the end. The fifteen years during which I studied the species comprises probably but a very small part of that period.

www.ingramcontent.com/pod-product-compliance
Lightning Source LLC
Chambersburg PA
CBHW032116280326
41933CB00009B/870